Everglades

By Janîce Leotti-Bachem

Consultant
Nanci R. Vargus, Ed.D.
Assistant Professor of Literacy
University of Indianapolis, Indianapolis, Indiana

Children's Press®
A Division of Scholastic Inc.
New York   Toronto   London   Auckland   Sydney
Mexico City   New Delhi   Hong Kong
Danbury, Connecticut

Designer: Herman Adler Design
Photo Researcher: Caroline Anderson
The photo on the cover shows the Everglades.

Library of Congress Cataloging-in-Publication Data

Leotti-Bachem, Janîce, 1962-
  Everglades / by Janîce Leotti-Bachem.
      p. cm. — (Rookie read-about geography)
   Includes bibliographical references and index.
   ISBN 0-516-22750-5 (lib. bdg.)   0-516-25929-6 (pbk.)
   1. Everglades (Fla.)—Juvenile literature. 2. Natural history—Florida—
Everglades—Juvenile literature. 3. Everglades National Park (Fla.)—Juvenile
literature. I. Title. II. Series.
   F317.E9L46 2005
   917.59'39—dc22

                              2004015560

CHILDREN'S PRESS, and ROOKIE READ-ABOUT®,
and associated logos are trademarks and or registered trademarks
of Scholastic Library Publishing. SCHOLASTIC and associated logos
are trademarks and or registered trademarks of Scholastic Inc.

1 2 3 4 5 6 7 8 9 10 R 14 13 12 11 10 09 08 07 06 05

Have you ever been to the Everglades?

Can you find the
Everglades on this map?

It is on the southern tip of
Florida.

ALABAMA

GEORGIA

ATLANTIC OCEAN

North
West — East
South

GULF OF MEXICO

F L O R I D A

Lake Okeechobee

Everglades

Everglades National Park

Florida Bay

CUBA

This land and water is part of Everglades National Park.

Part of the Everglades is
a national park.

National parks protect
land and animals. That
means plants and animals
are safe there.

People cannot build
homes or businesses in a
national park.

Ernest F. Coe helped to make the Everglades a national park.

Marjory Stoneman Douglas helped protect the Everglades, too. She wrote a book called *The Everglades: River of Grass*.

Marjory Stoneman Douglas is looking at grass.

Most people visit the Everglades in the summer.

There are two seasons in the Everglades.

It rains in the summer.
It is dry in the winter.

In the summer, it can rain up to 12 inches in one day!

Sawgrass grows in the
Everglades.

The gumbo-limbo tree grows in the Everglades, too. It has red bark that peels.

The manatee eats grasses and other plants in the Everglades.

Many animals live in the Everglades.

Some are endangered. That means they will become extinct (ek-STINGKT) if they are not protected.

The manatee is one animal that is endangered.

The Florida panther is also endangered.

There are less than fifty panthers in Florida.

Male American alligators are the largest reptiles in North America.

You can find alligators in the Everglades.

It does not rain much in the winter.

Water and food are hard to find. So, animals gather near water holes for food and water.

This alligator is in a water hole.

Many people visit the Everglades.

These people tour the Everglades in a boat.

Some visitors go to the Everglades to see the birds.

The Roseate spoonbill lives there. It has a beak shaped like a spoon.

These tires are polluting the water, or making it dirty.

The Everglades is in trouble.

Pollution has endangered the wildlife. Pollution harms plants and animals.

Marjorie Stoneman Douglas wrote, "There are no other Everglades in the world."

Telling people about the Everglades can help save this special place.

This is how the Everglades look from the sky.

Words You Know

alligator

Everglades National Park

Florida panther

gumbo-limbo tree

manatee

pollution

Roseate spoonbill

sawgrass

Index

About the Author

Janice Leotti-Bachem is a freelance writer and artist, and lives in New York with her husband. She loves animals, and enjoys taking care of two Jackson's chameleons, a lovebird, two newts, a toad, six anoles, a gecko, and a cat named Dizzy Mewler.

Photo Credits

Photographs © 2005: Corbis Images: 9 (Kevin Fleming), 25, 31 bottom left (George McCarthy); Getty Images/Tim Chapman/Liaison: 21, 30 top left; Minden Pictures/Fred Bavendam: 14, 31 top left; Nature Picture Library Ltd/Jeff Foott: cover; Peter Arnold Inc./Jim Wark: 29; Photo Researchers, NY: 17, 30 bottom left (Tom & Pat Leeson), 6, 30 top right (Jim Steinberg); PhotoEdit/Jeff Greenberg: 18; The Image Works: 26, 31 top right (Jeff Greenberg), 22 (Jason Laure); Tom Stack & Associates, Inc.: 10 (Larry Lipsky), 3 (David Young); Tony Arruza: 13, 30 bottom right; Visuals Unlimited/Maureen Burkhart: 12, 31 bottom right.

Maps by Bob Italiano